An AUDIENCE of ONE

The Purpose & Necessity of Prophetic Movement

An AUDIENCE *of* ONE

The Purpose & Necessity of Prophetic Movement

Scribal Prophet
Nabiyah Baht Yehuda

Seeing Is Believing

WHOLE WITHOUT A CRACK
PUBLICATIONS

An AUDIENCE *of* ONE

The Purpose & Necessity of Prophetic Movement

Copyright © 2012 by Nabiyah Baht Yehuda

Cover by: Angel Prints - info@angelprints.net

ISBN-13: 978-0-9834095-9-5

Book Website
www.ThoughtsFromTheThrone.VP.Web.com
Email: thescriptoriumofgod@aol.com

Printed by Whole Without A Crack Publications
www.wwacpselfpublishing.net Printed in U.S.A.

ACKNOWLEDGEMENTS

To the Lord first who allowed me to bear His Name and Who put this scroll in me and a dance in my heart. Thank you for allowing me to see through your life that all things are possible! To Apostle Patricia Wiley who allowed me to bloom as a butterfly and saw the best in me. To Betty Kiser for selling me my first flag and sowing 17 more into my ministry. To Jeraldine Council for saving as much of my poetry as possible. To my daughter, Serenity Blu, who is the crown of my life To Apostle Theresa Harvard Johnson for loving me with truth, believing in me, and knowing when to stand down and hear God concerning my life and call. Thank you for the release of the scribal anointing. I acknowledge Prophetess Sherry Wilson as a midwife and general in the spirit. Tabitha McGowan who sold me my first priestly garment. To Prophet Corinne Lawrence who has bloomed into an awesome woman of God. Finally this book is for every minister of dance who was misunderstood, made to feel uncertain, and walked alone, but still believed God.

For my mom: Ephesians 6:2 Honor (esteem and value as precious) your father and your mother—this is the first commandment with a promise.

Shalom Alechem to you all those who stood by me via Ruach Kodesh (Holy Spirit)

I pray for you...

Father, I pray for the eyes that will read this book. Put your word deep down on the inside of them and make them stand in it and for it. Increase them and set their feet in a large place. Cause them to know you in a greater measure. Walk with them when others want to walk away. Cause them to delight themselves in you, in the name of Yeshua (Jesus), Amen.

Are your garments white?

The wind of eternal change comes with revival on gusts
that cannot be stopped.
The wind carries in the midst of it a blast and a sound from Heaven
with wings on clouds filled with rain.
Promises from the throne…yes and established.

The mikvah…the bath of purification is needed to sanctify the body.
Yes the mayim chaim- living waters of which
no one will ever again thirst.
Prepare yourselves for the way of the Lord is set.
How does fire and wind hold Him up? How shall it uphold you?
It is the invisible word and the power of it.

Check your garments are they clean and unstained?
Check your speech is it clean and un-compromised?
Investigate, seek, and search out the inner man.
Has your spirit man slept in the temple malnourished?

The wind of eternal change comes with revival on gusts
that cannot be stopped.
The wind carries in the midst of it a blast and alarm from
Heaven with wings on clouds Filled with rain.
Promises from the throne…yes in victory.
The bride she hears and sees the cloud coming
with the invisible word and the power of it.

She sits on the rock with her lamp at her feet.
She is singing a psalm for her King…she is singing.
She hears and sees the cloud coming.
She feels the roll of the thunder and the shaking of the earth.
Are the guests ready?
Have they all received their invitations?
Behold, He comes.

TABLE OF CONTENTS

ACKNOWLEDGEMENTS 5

INTRODUCTION 9

MY CALL...13

COMMUNICATION......................................19

PRAYER & FASTING 25

SPIRITUAL MATURITY...................................31

EQUIPPING 42

ACTIVATION 44

WORSHIP 50

PROPHETIC MOVEMENT...............................65

EXERCISES 79

ABOUT THE AUTHOR 84

INTRODUCTION

Exodus 15:20 is a Hebrew Bible or Old Testament scripture concerning a woman known as Miriam. She was the sister of Moshe (Moses) and a prophetess. She led the other women into a worship and prophetic praise declaring what the Lord had done for them. Oh, what a mighty God we serve! She had the anointing and authority and her Pastor and brother backed her up in ministry. He supported what she was doing as she sang prophetically with passion while leading the other women into a victorious praise of what the Lord had just done. It is this leading and anointing that is imparted to us as well. It was not just a dance, but it was the word that accompanied the dance's rhythmic movements. Watch the incredible wave of glory in this passage.

"And Miriam the prophetess, the sister of Aaron, took a timbrel in her hand; and all the women went out after her with timbrels and danced. And Miriam answered them, "Sing ye to the Lord, for He hath triumphed gloriously: the horse and his rider hath he thrown into the sea."

This song and dance was a move. How? Well, let's take a look. She was in agreement with what the Lord had done. Miriam did not doubt the victory as some do. She not only believed it, she rejoiced in it, and put her faith to work by playing her timbrel to cause a sound in the atmosphere. It was the sound of victory as she led the other women into the same prophetic move and sound. There is power in agreement. There is power in movement.

Dancing is another way we celebrate God. It makes us feel good and it edifies our souls. It is a way of escape from depression, sadness, rejection, and many other emotions we go through. We are commanded to praise Him. We are made to praise His Name. He gives us the oil of joy for the spirit of heaviness. Prophetic dance is a word from Heaven and a yoke breaker. It is Isaiah chapters 60 and 61; it is John 10:10 and John 3:16 in motion. The Book of John says of Yeshua (Jesus), "and the word became flesh and dwelt among men." John 1:14 AMP version reads like this: *"And the word (Christ) became flesh (human, incarnate) and tabernacled (fixed his tent of flesh, lived awhile) among us; and we (actually) saw His glory (His honor, his majesty), such glory as an only begotten son receives from his father, full of grace (favor, lovingkindness) and truth."*

When we dance or move prophetically, the word in motion should become flesh and dwell among us and within us. It cannot just be a "dance." No, not in the way we have been taught it is. God is calling us into deeper waters. We are living and moving tabernacles with a charge to keep the fire burning. Leviticus 6:1213 says the priest is to put fire on the altar every morning and to burn up the fat of the peace offerings. Fat represents the excess things we do not need. In verse 13 the charge is: *"The fire shall be burning continually upon the altar; it shall not go out."*

Prophetic Dance is not a performance, but a consecrated life unto God. It is hearing His voice and following His steps from the spiritual realm into the natural. This is prophetic intercession, it is warfare, it is praise, it is prophetic movement. When other people see it they want to chime in and shout for joy as well. They want to war, they want to intercede and take part in whatever prophetic activity is going on at the moment. Dance tells a story and is inspiring. Ruach Kodesh (Holy Spirit) is a fire starter.

We must realize that when we offer our bodies as living sacrifices unto our God something happens. He is able to use us for His glory and He is able to reach people who may not hear Him in a traditional way. Some people can't really process the spoken word. They hear it, but for various reasons, it does not get all the way through to them. There may be some kind of emotional or spiritual block. These people cannot hear anything except music or movement. Holy Spirit will use this ministry as a piercing sound to break up the hardened hearts, tear down demonic strongholds, and translate us from one realm to another, to open our vision, and to resuscitate us in the spirit. I must sound the alarm to those who have this book in their hands. This is NOT a book on dancing. This scroll is about prophetic movement. If you desire to go into the chamber room of God and you want more of Him and not church/dance as usual, then eat this scroll for it will be sweet to you.

All glory to Yahweh for the many ways He speaks to us. When we submit to Him we have the power and the anointing to break yokes, lift burdens, and set the captives free, in the name of Yeshua HaMeshiach (Jesus the Christ) (Isaiah 61).

My prayer is that you are prayerful going into this or any ministry. It is a call and not just something to do to pass the time. This is not a performance in the sense of entertaining people. It is not just dance; it's the word of El Elyon (The Most High God). This is God performing and demonstrating His hand, thought, will and heart in the earth realm. Adonai is calling the 'whosever will' vessel.

You will see where I put Holy Spirit rather than THE Holy Spirit. I explain this so that as you read you do not think it to be an error.

Holy Spirit is a person, specifically of the 3 fold personage of God. We do not say, "The Jesus." I pray you hear and understand this. May the Lord bless you. (Shalom. Be entire and complete)

MY CALL

When I was first asked to minister in dance I thought it was a joke. I had only been saved for a short time when my spiritual mom said that my Apostle wanted me to minister in dance. All the way home on the bus I thought to myself, "Are they kidding me?" I mean, what did I know about it? I danced around at home, but I never told a soul. I was in a five-fold ministry and was still learning what that meant. I was just beginning my relationship with the Lord putting as much road between myself and sin as possible. I was getting up around 4 or 5am to spend time with the Lord in prayer because even though I did not know a lot, I knew I wanted as much of Him as I could get. I didn't even know why, but I did. I would put on a worship cd and just dance. It all came naturally. Little did I know it was a Holy Ghost set-up. Every time I lifted my hands there was a clink in the spirit. There was another part of me I was surrendering. Ruach Kodesh (Holy Spirit) was doing something in me and taking me to a place I had not known before.

When I finally made it home, changed out of my church clothes, and got comfortable on my bed, I looked out of the window and it hit me. "They are not asking me to dance, Lord...You are." Immediately I told the Lord I was sorry. I also was afraid because my private worship was going to be on display. Yes, I was afraid, but the fire of Ruach Kodesh (Holy Spirit) pushed me. I am a creative person and very revealing with my facial expressions. I talked a lot with my hands and the

Ruach Kodesh (Holy Spirit) was going to use it to communicate the words God was speaking to me and why not? Deaf and mute people communicate with their hands, bodies, and facial expressions to get their point across all the time.

I was still wet behind the ears in the spirit. I was innocent in that arena, but perhaps it was why He decided to use me. I had been rejected in the church. No one understood me and it seemed no one cared to understand. I was not like everyone else and did not dress like they did. I was usually alone. Most people would say hello, but they did not really want to know me except maybe to get some personal information. They wanted information to spread throughout the church among themselves, I never understood how they could do such a thing in church of all places. Nevertheless, I was so hungry for God that I just kept coming back and I ate all I could stand as far as the Word was concerned. The church may not have wanted me, but God did. He had a plan, purpose, and a love He wanted to get to me and through me. You see, I had been broken and He wanted to heal me. I had been depleted and He wanted to restore me. I had been misused and He wanted to use me for His glory. He wanted to give me beauty for ashes and mold me in the faces of my enemies. God had a plan to use me as an inspiration not only in the church, but also in the world. Besides, we are commanded to love.

Leviticus 19:1 KJV

Do not seek revenge or bear a grudge against one of your people, but love your neighbor as yourself. I am the Lord.

15   *SCRIBAL PROPHET NABIYAH BAHT YEHUDA*

The second thing I had to remember is that Yeshua (Jesus) was also rejected, but He loved ANYWAY.

After realizing what God wanted me to do, I went running around Manhattan trying to find something to wear to minister in for the service. At the time I did not know it was called ministering, I just thought it was dancing. I was nervous, scared, and had no idea what I was supposed to do, what I was going to do and how I could possibly get out of it. I had not grown up in church. I became saved when I was thirty-five years old. I knew I could not lie about why I couldn't do it. I was trapped and decided to search out dance stores around the city. None of them had praise dance outfits, but then I never saw one to know the difference. Now that I think about it, Holy Spirit knew they did not have what I needed, so I left empty handed. Eventually, I had to put together pieces from various stores. I felt like my skirt should be wide and my blouse or top should have bell sleeves. I found something and bought it from a department store. It was all white and I would have to make do with it.

When the day came for me to get out there, I was a mess emotionally and wanted to cry, but I had to get over myself. I had heard that one of the ministers' mom had passed so I used a song by Aretha Franklin and Dennis Edwards (from the Temptations) called "A song for you." It was a sweet song and I dedicated it to her. I cannot say that I recall how everything went. They probably clapped because it was my first time and thought I did not know I was supposed to use a church song. I originally did have a "church song." The words of the song I used said, "We are alone now and I'm singing this song to you. You gave me precious secrets *(and I held my Bible up)* with the

Truth, withholding nothing…you came out in front while I was hiding." Now doesn't that sound like a mom and daughter thing? It made me think about a little child hiding behind his or her mommy's skirt. It made me think about all the things a mom would share with a child.

Well, I know that God CAN take a secular song and sing it to us as long as it is not fleshy. That was the only secular song I have ever done up until this day. We will talk more about this later.

When I tell you I was in church five minutes, I mean I knew nothing. I had never been to a church except that one. I got saved on the same day I visited that little church in Brooklyn. They hijacked me in less than a year to minister in dance. I had never been to church except when my mom took us for Easter when we were children. I did not remember anything that was said, all I knew was that I was getting a new dress and shoes for Easter. It was the only thing I found exciting about church. I was young and I don't recall even hearing about Yeshua (Jesus). Sometimes I wonder if they even had an altar call or if my mom heard it. I do remember when I was little that she would say the Lord's Prayer. I'm sure it was because of those prayers that I believed in God, but He was the "Unknown God" because I had no intimate knowledge of Him. I said grace and thanked Him for the food sometimes, but did not know who He was. I thanked and praised Him every now and then because He knew my name, who I was and He had a plan for my life. Now there I was dancing for Him.

HE Called…

I always danced around the house as a young girl and was taken one day by my mom to the Alvin Ailey Dance School. I was intimidated, insecure, and afraid. I thought I could not do all those moves I saw them doing and no one encouraged me to stay and learn. I just wanted to go home. Fear did all the talking for me then. Sometimes I think I wish I would have stayed, but this is just more glory that is ascribed to the Lord. He would teach me

Himself. He would dress me and tell me what music to use, then lead and guide me with His eye. He did all this after I was saved.

God never took away my desire to dance because it was what He called me to do. The enemy tried to discourage me and fill me with fear, but I am here to tell you sons and daughters of God that what God has purposed for you to do no one can lay a claim on and no one can take it away. While dancing around the house as a little girl, the Lord was watching over His word and performing it prophetically. No matter who said what, THAT word was going to be revealed in me. He grew in me and matured me in the dance until one day it hit me.

I was sitting on the pulpit one day after service and told my Apostle Patricia, "I realized the other day that I am not dancing, I am ministering." She threw her hands up in the air and said, "Yes!" This began my prophetic movement journey and Ruach Kodesh began to expand my vocabulary in the spirit through ONmy body. This earthen vessel had a voice, an assignment, and a prophetic move of God. I had the name for my ministry:

COMMUNICATION

How Elohim communicates to us

Abba communicates to and through us via Ruach Kodesh. Ruach Kodesh is Hebrew (Ivreet) for Holy Spirit. Ruach Kodesh speaks to us in a variety of ways. It is the spirit of counsel and wisdom as well. Whenever the Lord is speaking to us, He chooses the way in which to get His message across. He will do it via dreams, visions, a small still voice in our spirit, or in an audible voice. He can speak to us directly or through another human vessel. He can also speak through dance. He spoke to Balaam through a mule. He is sovereign which means He can do whatever He likes at any time. We are the ones who have to take the limits off and not box Him in. We serve a limitless God and His desire is to see us walk, move, and flow in liberty. Proverbs 3:5 tells us not to lean on our own understanding.

Whenever we see a praise dance it should excite us and lead us into praise as well.

It should stir up something within us because He is our God and He has done something for us. His banner over us is love (Song of Solomon 2:4). He is worthy of all our praise. Let everything that has breathe praise the Lord. His Name is Elohay tahee la tee, interpreted God of my praise (Psalm 109:1).

We should know and be intimate with the Father and if you haven't been in that place, then you are really missing out on something. He calls us into intimacy because we are the Church, the Bride of Christ, and He is the Groom. In a natural marriage the groom and the bride are intimate and become one. Oneness, unity, and harmony are what Yeshua prayed about in the New Testament. He also said He and the Father are one. In Hebrew, this is Echud not the number one. Echud is about unity. If we are one or in harmony with Him, there is very little room for confusion or mistakes. He wants the sound of Heaven coming to and through us. Then we can communicate it to the world and to other believers in Christ.

When it comes to hearing from God and discerning the sound of Heaven and relaying it to someone else, we must be careful. We must also be full of faith and confident that we know His voice and His heart. It should all line up with the scriptures. God never ever contradicts His written word. To do so would lead to confusion. If God contradicted His own word, how could we then rely on Him or His word?

When the Lord says, *"Dance for me,"* What do you say if you never heard Him speak something like this to you? Of course we want to question it, but it is scriptural. We cannot argue with scripture. As His sheep, you have to get to know His Voice.

Any man that comes to God must first believe He is a rewarder of them that diligently seek Him. This means we must lend ourselves to prayer. We must communicate with Him. It's all about getting to know each other. After all, isn't that what people do in relationships? We are in a relationship. He has asked for our hand in marriage and we said yes. Our yes must be consistent and founded in humility, trust, and love.

Let's look at some examples of communication with the Father.

There is something called the law of first mention. Whenever we see something in the Bible for the first time, we should pay attention to it because it is significant. The first time we see communication with the Father is in the book of Genesis (Berishit- pronounced, berehsheet). This is God the Father as a provider:

Genesis 1:27-29 KJV

So God created man in his own image, in the image of God created he him; male and female created he them. And God blessed them, and God said unto them, Be fruitful, and multiply, and replenish the earth, and subdue it: and have dominion over the fish of the sea, and over the fowl of the air, and over every living thing that moveth upon the earth. And God said, Behold, I have given you every herb bearing seed, which is upon the face of all the earth, and every tree, in the which is the fruit of a tree yielding seed; to you it shall be for meat.

The above scripture is an illustration of God as the Father and the Father as our Provider. In the garden, they were provided with everything they needed, just as it is with us now. All we need to do is BELIEVE that He gives us what we need before we need it. We have to open our spiritual eyes and look around. Now, let's talk about the faith that connects with the spiritual eyes.

FAITH

Romans 12:6 KJV
Having then gifts differing according to the grace that is given to us, whether prophecy, let us prophesy according to the proportion of faith;

Having different gifts according to the grace that is given to YOU!
Don't try to be like anyone else. Work what He gave you!

James 1:6-7 KJV
But let him ask in faith, nothing wavering. For he that wavereth is like a wave of the sea driven with the wind and tossed. For let not that man think that he shall receive any thing of the Lord.

Many will see someone minister in dance and wish they could do it. You can dance! We are all made to worship Him! Don't doubt, just move!

Faith in action

James 2:17
Even so faith, if it hath not works, is dead, being alone.

Faith in English is an abstract word. Let's use the Hebrew term which is concrete, ne-eman. It means secure like a peg and firm. That is concrete. This is the word they use for faith or faithful. We must then be firm and secure because if we are not, we will have nothing to hold our ministry to. Remember the clothes line used to hang up your clothes outside? You put the peg there so it won't fall to the ground and get dirty. All the hard work of getting your clothes clean would be for nothing because you would have to go wash them all again if the clothes were not securely and firmly put in place by the peg. Do you get the picture?

Matthew 17:20

And Jesus said unto them, Because of your unbelief: for verily I say unto you, If ye have faith as a grain of mustard seed, ye shall say unto this mountain, Remove hence to yonder place; and it shall remove; and nothing shall be impossible unto you.

With prophetic movement as in all things that we do must be fueled by what we say we believe. The Bible says that God watches over His word to perform it. And so likewise as we are perfumed by Ruach Kodesh and we are examining our ministries, fasting, praying, seeking Ruach Kodesh, eating of the good scroll of life, there should be some evidence. Miracles and signs follow those who believe. I think the problem is that the word believe is yet another abstract word with no real meaning. Hebrew is a concrete language. Let us use the word translated for believe. This word means support. So we don't say we believe God, but we support Him. When someone supports you, you see some type of evidence and also this takes the responsibility off of God and puts it on US. God does not have do any more proving. It is us who have to move in what we say we support. When someone is running for office they have supporters, not believers. The supporters are out campaigning and telling others about this candidate and how much this person has done and what they will do. These supporters are out and about doing the business of making a sound and moving in such a way that all they do is represent the person and NOT themselves. The level of support we show for the Lord causes things to move--nothing is impossible.

JUST DO IT!

PRAYER & FASTING

Acts 6:4

But we will give ourselves continually to prayer, and to the ministry of the word.

Matthew 17:21

But this kind does not go out except by prayer and fasting.

Without the word of God and prayer in us, we have NO ministry. What we will have will only be recognized as entertainment. We are not here to entertain, but to minister. I cannot stress this enough. There are many entertainers in the church and those who seriously hear the call to ministry must discern the difference. We want to hear from the throne room of Yehova and rightly discern.

We give ourselves to prayer because it is how we communicate with Him. Keeping an open line of communication is imperative. He wants us to hear from Him just as much as He wants to hear from us. This is a vital part of ministry. This is how ministry is birthed and we receive direction. No one can fuel his or her ministry themselves. We want God to breathe on (inspire) our ministry where He is calling ALL the shots. He is the One Who knows, sees, and runs it all.

When I became a bit more matured in the Lord, I would go to the Church or wherever it was I was called to minister and I would sit alone in a room away from everyone else until it was time for me to minister. At this time I needed to do it because quite honestly, I was easily distracted by conversation. I needed to be in a place to hear Him. Maybe He wanted to change the song or give me a specific prophetic motion to execute. All I knew was that I was afraid to get out there on my own. I always found myself nervous although it never showed on the outside. I would pray and meditate on the song and whatever it was He wanted me to do. Some don't have to do this and some just don't do it, but they should. When I say some don't do this, I am saying that some folks get a song of their own choosing and they wear whatever they want to. They begin to go off in their own spirits. The ministry of prophetic movement has not been taken seriously and pushed back for years. No one wants to hear from the prophet. No one wants correction, they only want the blessings of God, but the Bible says that the beginning of wisdom is the fear of the Lord. Wisdom, in this ministry, will speak to you and tell you to turn down your plate because the atmosphere you are going into is going to require more of the Spirit of God and less of you. This atmosphere will have demonic influence and warfare and your flesh is not what pulls it down because it is only through God that strongholds are brought down.

Fasting is an integral part of prophetic movement because of these things I mentioned. The scripture said that THESE KIND only come out through fasting and prayer. We cannot get around protocol. If God took His hand away, the devil would surely kill us. In the army there is a ranking system and there is a protocol. If you are in the army you will learn the system and it will be a part of your life. You will eat, sleep, and drink protocol because if you don't, you are out. Fasting is hard to do because sometimes our god can be our bellies. Self-denial is not in our DNA therefore, we have such a hard time telling it whether or not we can have certain things or nothing at all. No, this is not easy, but it is a part of the mentor program in the Holy Ghost. We have to become lean, mean fighting machines in the realm of the spirit. The enemy knows our weaknesses and will feed them and like a snake, the more you feed it, the bigger it gets.

Prayer is your communication not with Father, but with Ruach Kodesh. That is your counselor whom Yeshua said He would send after He departed.

John 14:26 NIV
But the Counselor, the Holy Spirit, whom the Father will send in my name, will teach you all things and will remind you of everything I have said to you.

Yeshua said He would not speak much with the disciples in John 14:30

Acts 13:2-4
While they were worshiping the Lord and fasting, the Holy Spirit said, Separate now for Me Barnabas and Saul for the work to which I have called them.

When we fast and get into the presence of the Lord, He separates us for Himself and brings us into a place where He can reveal things. It is in this place that we learn our true purpose. There are many people telling us how we should do this and do that. My question is, *are you going to set the opinion and counsel of people above the counsel of the Lord?* Father really does know best!

Acts 13:3-4 AMP
Then after fasting and praying, they put their hands on them and sent them away. So then, being sent out by the Holy Spirit, they went down to Seleucia, and from [that port] they sailed away to Cyprus.

It is after and even during fasting and praying that we can hear and get direction from Adonai (Lord) via Ruach Kodesh. As we prepare for ministry we wash ourselves in the word of God. We pray, fast, and eat the scroll, that is, eat the word. Without it we can do nothing. We must stay connected to the vine because He is the one who sends us out. What He is doing is putting an assignment in us and giving directions and instructions on how to carry out this assignment. Every assignment changes and what He gives us to do is a different MOVEMENT.

John 15:1-5 AMP
I AM the True Vine, and My Father is the Vine dresser.

Allow Him to dress you. We cannot keep choosing what we want to wear and think, *"Oh, this looks nice."* Is the garment you picked what He is saying?

John 15:2 KJV
Any branch in Me that does not bear fruit [that stops bearing] He cuts away (trims off, takes away); and He cleanses and repeatedly prunes every branch that continues to bear fruit, to make it bear more and richer and more excellent fruit.

Identity

Who are you and what kind of fruit are you bearing? We are made in His image and He knows the seeds of greatness that He has put inside you and I and He knows what fruit is supposed to come forth. Identity is important. We must know who HE says that we are and adhere to that or what you produce will not be an acceptable offering. Ask Cain in Genesis, chapter 4.

John 15:3 AMP
You are cleansed and pruned already, because of the word which I have given you [the teachings I have discussed with you].

Cleansed and identified

In the old testament before the priest came into the temple to minister they had to wash their hands and feet. They could not go into the temple to do the assignments without being clean (kosher). Exodus 30:17-21 explains about the bronze laver the Lord told Moshe to tell his brother Aaron and his sons to wash in before they went in to minister and that this was a statute forever. In this dispensation our bronze laver is the word of God and Ruach Kodesh is inspecting us to see what we are bringing before the altar.

John 15:4-5 AMP
Dwell in Me, and I will dwell in you. [Live in Me, and I will live in you.] Just as no branch can bear fruit of itself without abiding in (being vitally united to) the vine, neither can you bear fruit unless you abide in Me. I am the Vine; you are the branches. Whoever lives in Me and I in him bears

much (abundant) fruit. However, apart from Me [cut off from vital union with Me] you can do nothing'

Let us all do what we know to do in His strength, power, and by His Spirit. It is according to the power working within us. Staying connected to the vine is the only choice we have for bearing good fruit that will not only remain, but reproduce. We are before the door (Yeshua) with our ministry and the laver (wash basin) was positioned there at the door of the Holy place and the altar. Let's get clean of opinions, sin, attitudes, condemnation, confusion, entertainment, compromise, comparison, and anything else distracting us from Christ and our purpose.

All of this word lays down a solid foundation. You cannot move prophetically without the word and the Spirit of God that leads you into the places you should go. You are sent, but not sent everywhere. We have to hear, be mature enough to listen, and receive our assignments. Even the army, navy, and marines are not sent into every situation.

SPIRITUAL MATURITY

Maturity in discerning

We have to be accurate in all we do and we must do it in Him and not in ourselves. We are to be mature and not wishy washy in this walk. There are many who come to deceive and are deceived themselves. If we do not grow up and discern rightly, we too will fall in the wake of deception separating ourselves from truth. Remember, He said, *"My sheep know My voice and a stranger they will not follow."*

John 10:26 ESV says, *The sheep that are My own hear and are listening to My voice; and I know them, and they follow Me.*

John 10:3-5 AMP
The watchman opens the door for this man, and the sheep listen to his voice and heed it; and he calls his own sheep by name and brings (leads) them out. When he has brought his own sheep outside, he walks on before them, and the sheep follow him because they know his voice. They will never [on any account] follow a stranger, but will run away from him because they do not know the voice of strangers or recognize their call.

This is powerful. If we can only get a righteous understanding of this scripture and allow it to become flesh and dwell with us. We must understand that Holy Spirit is the watchman and we are the sheep of Gods' pasture. Sheep only follow the shepherd and they follow and trust in him because they are familiar with his voice. Familiar comes from the word family. We are in the family of Eloheinu (Our God) and we should never follow the voice of a stranger. A stranger is someone not in the family and someone we do not know. To know means to be intimate with or close enough to see eye to eye. This is not the English word know as in head knowledge. Ruach Kodesh is wanting us to draw near enough to see wisdom, love, maturity, grace, and Yeshua eye to eye.

There is a call going out not just from Heaven, but from the camp of the enemy. Sawtahn (Satan) has ministers as well. In maturity, we must discern who is speaking and the movement going on in the realm of the spirit.

We cannot afford to be immature in the things of God. We have to fine tune our hearing, discernment (understanding), and spiritual perception. It is time to leave the elementary things and get off the milk and sit down for meat. It is time to grow up in God.

What does this have to do with dance? Everything. Especially prophetic dance because you are a dancing preacher. You are an oracle of God in motion and the rhema word being manifested. You have been given a charge to proclaim His great gospel. Speaking for Him in motion.

The eagle is the symbol for the prophetic. Watch this: The eagle is faster in flight (movement) and its eyes are six times sharper than human eyes. It has what is known as binocular eyesight to help them gauge distances and project outward and forward so that there is an overlapping of vision. It can spot its prey from hundreds of yards away. The bald eagle's head can turn up to a 270 degree angle. The retina of the bald eagle is far superior to that of a human and it has a retina made like cones to recognize color and rods to recognize light. When they are born their eyes are brown, but when they mature the eyes turn to a bright yellow (glory). Even the eagles' eyebrows offer them protection and security against injury and shields the eyes from the glare of the sun. It also has nictitating (an eye that opens and closes quickly like a wink) membranes which allow them to look directly into the sun, if they must, in order to spot prey. I can say more about this awesome bird, but I just want to make a point of the changes Ruach Kodesh takes us through. It's the process of going from one level to another; from the natural to the spiritual and from the shallow waters into the greater depths in Him.

There are those who stand for truth (God) and those who stand for lies (Sawtahn/Satan). We cannot stand up to minister before the people with contamination brought on by sin, rebellion, and disobedience. These are considered the fruit of Sawtahn. We are to desire to walk in the Spirit of God and be mature in Him. What are you standing on and for? Let a man so examine himself, ministry included. When one moves in sin, it is like a cloak, and there is an aroma to it. When you stand before God and His congregation there will be a stench. It is called a fly in the ointment.

Ecclesiastes 10:1 AMP

Dead flies cause the ointment of the perfumer to putrefy and send forth a vile odor; so does a little folly (in him who is valued for wisdom) outweigh wisdom and honor.

Let's take a quick dip in the scroll for a moment...

Side bar

An apothecary (raw-kawk in Hebrew) is a perfumer. A perfumer is someone who prepares spices. Biblically these were those who were charged to make the holy oil. This is not a light thing. This was heavy in that according to Exodus 30:22-28, Moshe (Moses) was given a charge from the Lord to prepare the oil, what spices to use and how much. Moshe used the mixture to anoint the ark of the testimony, the altar of incense, the altar for burnt offering, the laver and so on. This oil was costly and special. It was not for everything or everyone.

We cannot take this precious oil (anointing) and smear it where ever, whenever and however we want to. We cannot be in a mess and call it blessed. This is perversion and a stench will have gone up to the nostrils of the Holy One.

In Exodus 30:34-38, God clarifies that there is a certain oil only for the priests and it was not to be duplicated. No one can duplicate the anointing that God has put in you. God is sovereign, He can duplicate or impart what He likes into a set people. It is HE who sets the standards and HE is the Apothecary. What He charges us to do that shall we do in the way HE desires it to be done. I pray that I am clear in this portion of the sefer scroll (book). He loves us with an everlasting love and has a portion in all of us that will be an everlasting anointing. Let's not waste it or the time He has given us to understand and put to use for His honor and glory. Let His truth be a lamp at our feet and a light along the pathway He has set for us.

Tehillim **Psalm 119:105 NIV**
Your word is a lamp to my feet and a light for my path.

Apostle Patricia always encouraged me. It took her loving eye to see what the Lord was doing. I had some bumps and learned a lot in the process of maturing. The Lord taught me to fast and pray and to wait on Him and His leading. I am still learning; learning does not cease. Ruach Kodesh is our constant teacher as long as we live and are submitted.

It was funny how every time I tried to choreograph something He would change it and I could not do what I thought I was going to do. I began to just sit and listen to the music, meditating on the words. They would speak to my heart about who He was or the state of the church or it could have been some emotional upheaval the Lord wanted to minister to. Finally I was learning His name and what it really meant. I was maturing in Him and learning about intimacy and His response to what myself and anyone else was going through.

Matthew 5:48
Be ye therefore perfect, even as your Father which is in Heaven is perfect.

This word perfect is talking about maturity, not flawlessness. We all come with and will leave this earth with flaws. This scripture is basically saying, just do what He asks you to do with reverence, a good attitude, and zeal. It also means to be a grown up about it. We complain and grumble way too much. Let us be more like Yeshua.

1 Corinthians 14:20

Brethren, be not children in understanding: howbeit in malice be ye children, but in understanding be men.

We have to be as innocent as children not knowing anything about maliciousness and in understanding be mature as I stated earlier. This is to understand what your call and purpose is and get busy doing it. We do not have the time nor should we give our energy to foolishness, fights, quarrels, or gossip. This can hinder your ministry. Do not worry what someone else is doing. Scrutinize yourself and go on and grow in God.

There has been a charge from Heavens' throne room to equip the saints of Yahweh and prepare the way of the Lord. Christ is soon to return and we must posture ourselves to hear from Him and His Spirit alone. He uses various ways to communicate to us and it is His prerogative which way He chooses. It is our responsibility to hear and see what He is saying to us and relay it to the people.

Prerogative is defined as an exclusive or special right, power or privilege as one belonging to an office or an official body; one belonging to a person, group, or class of individuals or one possessed by a nation as an attribute of sovereignty. Don't you just love it? It's for us to understand that we can see the weight of His word, His office, and His sovereignty and how we should respond.

Habakkuk 2:1 KJV

I will stand upon my watch, and set me upon the tower, and will watch to see what he will say unto me, and what I shall answer when I am reproved.

Standing on your watch is a prophetic move even though you are standing. You are not just standing although it may look like it from the outside. You are listening, you are praying. Prophetic movement is as simple as taking a pen to paper to record the word of the Lord. This is what scribes did and do. Especially prophetic scribes. They record, announce, publish, and proclaim His word. Someone will see it, hear it and they will experience it. The prophetic movement positions you and sets you in a place. Everyone has a different place in a different season.

Communicate - to transmit information, thought, or feeling so that it is satisfactorily received or understood. a: to convey knowledge of or information about: make known. to cause (something) to pass from one to another.

Remember I said that the mute have a way of communicating with their hands and such. Well, let us look into the word. We can find all types of scriptures where the men of God where told to do such and such a thing.

Moshe held his arms up and they won the battle, but when his hands went down they lost (Exodus 17:11). When the Lord told him to stretch out his rod, the sea parted. Aaron stretched out the rod and his hand and struck the dust of the ground and gnats came upon men and animals in Egypt (Exodus 8:17).

Yeshua told the man to stretch out his shriveled hand and it was healed. Before the Lord gave him direction, he could not do it (Mark 3:3-5)

In II Kings 4:43 the Prophet Elisha fed 100 men with 20 loaves of bread with some heads of grain. His servant asked how were they going to do this and Elisha said to set it before them and there will be some left over and there were according to the word of the Lord. They had to move prophetically. They had to do what was told and that brought increase.

Ezekiel 4:4 - This prophet was told to lay on his side for 390 days and to put the sin of the house of Israel upon himself. This was a prophetic act. Please read the whole chapter to see this amazing move of God.

Prophesying is a prophetic movement- speaking over dead bones and speaking over the atmosphere to stop the rain. These are miracles and signs following them that believe God!

Cowd - In the Hebrew from Jeremiah 23:18 means "a session" or a "company of persons in close deliberation." It implies intimacy, as in secret consultation.

Jeremiah 23:18 CJB

But which of them has been present at Adonai's counsel to see and hear His word? Who has paid attention to his word enough to hear it?

Jeremiah 23:18 AMP

For who among them has stood in the council of the Lord, that he should perceive and hear His word? Who has marked His word [noticing and observing and giving attention to it] and has [actually] heard it?

Faith - Without question. Belief and trust in and loyalty to God (2): belief in the traditional doctrines of a religion b (1): firm belief in something for which there is no proof (2): complete trust.

Reminder: Please note that the Hebrew word for faith is interpreted as support. We don't just say we have faith for we know that devils also believe. We say we support God which now puts the responsibility on us to DO SOMETHING to prove it.

Synonyms for Faith: adhesion, allegiance, attachment, commitment, constancy, dedication, devotedness, devotion, faith, faithfulness, fastness, fealty, loyalty, piety, steadfastness, troth

Related Words for faith: affection, fondness; determination, firmness, resolution; dependability, reliability, trustability, trustiness, trustworthiness.

We cannot shrink back and be afraid of what He is calling us to do. It will take faith, trust, love, support, and hearing from Holy Spirit. He is calling us into new territories where we have not gone before, but He acts as a cloud by day and a fire by night to guide us.

Abba does not do anything without purpose, nor does He give us things spiritual or natural for no good reason. He is the Master of legions. He is tactical and on purpose. Are we not made in His image? There are several scriptural reasons on why He would endow us with the gift of dance. We are His children and He wants us to have spiritual gifts. He uses us as banners;

He uses us as His word in motion to evangelize, encourage, intercede, and bring joy to those who are not just in the household of faith, but to those in the outer court.

1. Cultivate the gift in discerning- Being mature
Hebrews 5:14 KJV
But strong meat belongeth to them that are of full age, even those who by reason of use have their senses exercised to discern both good and evil.

2. Intercede
Romans 1:9 KJV
For God is my witness, whom I serve with my spirit in the gospel of his Son, that without ceasing I make mention of you always in my prayers.

In prophetic movement we are in a state of intercession before we arrive to someone's church or event. Have you been to the nursing home or a school? Yes, you are moving and interceding for those that are in that place. As you spin, and you shake your hand and as you use whatever He leads you to as a tool (ex: flags, banners, shofar, ribbons, and or garments in a certain color)

Colossians 1:9 KJV

For this cause we also, since the day we heard it, do not cease to pray for you, and to desire that ye might be filled with the knowledge of his will in all wisdom and spiritual understanding.

EQUIPPING

Why we need to be equipped

Ephesians 4:7, 11-12 KJV

But unto every one of us is given grace according to the measure of the gift of Christ. And he gave some, apostles; and some, prophets; and some, evangelists; and some, pastors and teachers; For the perfecting of the saints, for the work of the ministry, for the edifying of the body of Christ.

I am in love with these verses. Please look this up in the Amplified Bible for greater clarity. It clearly lets us know that all ministries, regardless of denomination, are always to edify, set free, and mature the people of God and not to entertain. I repeat this throughout the scroll. Please notice how it says some are Apostle, some are prophets, some are evangelist and some are pastors, but when you get to teachers it just says and teachers. We are all to teach regardless of what office or ministry we stand in. If you are telling yourself, "I could never teach anyone how to…." this scripture is for you. I never saw myself in a place of teaching till Ruach Kodesh gave me a vision of me playing school when I was eight years old. I played the teacher. I was bent over in a room after ministering in prophetic movement. I was led up there by someone and left alone in the room and I cried and cried. I began speaking in the Spirit and He kept saying, "Morah, morah!" In Hebrew it means teacher. I looked up and saw a black board and looked around the room to find that I was in a classroom! I did not know this church had a class room. I was so deep in the Spirit of worship

I did not know where they had taken me. Of the many rooms they had, this is where they brought me. I am sharing this with you because as I write, Holy Spirit is directing me according to who He knows will read this.

This portion of the scroll is not by accident or coincidence. By the way, In Hebrew there is no word for coincidence. Everything is pre-ordained including your eyes seeing this book.

God wants to do something new in you, shall you not know it? He wants to shift some things around in you and awaken something that He has placed deep down on the inside of you. He wants to move you to move something in the atmosphere. He wants to catapult you in to a higher place in order to change your view, but you have to change the view on the level you are on in order to see the vast and great thing He wants to show you beloved. I think this is a perfect place for you to put the book down and go on your face. Ask Him some questions and let Him minister to you. Don't worry, the book will be here when you get back. Your prophetic movement is to go down on the floor. Remember, that is where His feet are. That is how you follow.

ACTIVATION

Why does He want us to be activated?

1 Timothy 1:6 AMP

That is why I would remind you to stir up (rekindle the embers of, fan the flame of, and keep burning) the [gracious] gift of God, [the inner fire] that is in you by means of the laying on of my hands with those of the elders at your ordination].

Mattiyahu (Matthew) 4:17-24

*From that time Jesus began to preach, and to say, **Repent**: for the kingdom of Heaven is at hand. And Jesus, walking by the sea of Galilee, saw two brethren, Simon **called** Peter, and Andrew his brother, casting a net into the sea: for they were fishers. And he saith unto them, **Follow me**, and **I will make you** fishers of men. And they straightway left their nets, and followed him. And going on from thence, he saw other two brethren, James the son of Zebedee, and John his brother, in a ship with Zebedee their father, mending their nets; and he **called** them. And they immediately left the ship and their father, and followed him. And Jesus went about all Galilee, **teaching** in their synagogues, and preaching the gospel of the kingdom, and healing all manner of sickness and all manner of disease among the people. And his fame went throughout all Syria: and they brought unto him all sick people that were taken with divers diseases and torments, and those which were possessed with devils, and those which were lunatic, and those that had the palsy; and he **healed** them.*

I have made certain words bold to highlight the order and the assignment. Our first thing before we go forth in anything is repentance. After we have lifted ourselves up off the floor and picked up the mirror (Bible) again to have another look we notice that it really is the Lord who calls us. We don't call ourselves. It is He who will make us and not we ourselves. Our answer is to follow Him, not a fad, tradition, or anyone else. Apostle Paul said, *"Follow me as I follow Christ."* If you have a mentor that you follow and they are submitted to the Ruach (Spirit) of God, then you are by default following HaMeshiach (The Messiah).

Next, the ministry is to teach and preach the gospel of the Kingdom, after which healing comes. My question is, is this what happens in your ministry? If not, you have to ask yourself why not? It is only the anointing that breaks yokes, it is only the anointing written in the scroll portion of Isaiah 61 that makes one able to preach, to loose the captive, to reconcile, and restore a soul to soundness and oneness in God.

Yeshua (Jesus) is our example. He has called us into ministry to glorify Him. We have the ministry of reconciliation. We are called by His Name to do great exploits in and for the kingdom of Yahweh. He said that we would do greater things so expect it and look for it. We have to understand that dance is like any other ministry, it is a call. He calls us into relationship with Him and He calls us to purpose and destiny. He is calling us as the saved to serve and to become co-laborers with Him in setting the captives free. Isaiah 61 is a mandate. It is the anointing to bring liberty to those who have been held captive, those in bondage, and to give the blind their sight back. This ministry is called to restore. If Yeshua (Jesus) is our example then it is our responsibility to study His walk and we are called to walk in this same way.

He did not come to entertain anyone, but to edify, exhort, heal, restore, mend, and rescue those that are lost and dying. This is what we must remember more than anything else. If you find that you love the praise of man rather than God, prophetic dance is not for you. If you find that you want to "dance" rather than minister you should reconsider, investigate, and sit down for a season and examine your motives. Again, this is a consecrated lifestyle. For me, this is my worship poured out on Him. If I never minister in the church, hospital, or anywhere else He has sent me, I would still be at home at various hours of the day or night honoring Him through the ministry of dance and prophetic movement. I have clapped my hands, picked up my staff, waved my banner and no one was around to see it, but something happened. It is what I did before He set me before the people. Know and be sure this is the mandate from Heaven concerning your ministry work. You must make your election sure and walk worthy of your calling. This is only one of the gifts of the Spirit of God. Just as He has many names depicting His different characteristics, this is another one from the same Spirit. Please do not misunderstand, we are all called to worship Him. It does not take a special anointing to worship, but it does take RELATIONSHIP. I am only separating for the purpose of you knowing and discerning the difference in "dance" ministries.

When I say dance ministries I mean those that are not prophetic in nature and there is no assignment as that a five-fold ministry would have. Praise dance groups do just that, they praise. THERE IS NOTHING WRONG WITH THAT.

I want to clarify that when the prophetic oil is poured out it is for change. Anything I do is out of my office. Because I am a prophet, my "dance," teaching, prophesying, and preaching will always be out of my office. It is the same with an Apostle and those functioning in other offices. Ministry gifts and offices are not the same. Someone can be prophetic, but it does not make them a prophet. You can have an apostolic anointing, but it does not make you an Apostle. The gift of prophecy can flow as Ruach wills and if you are in prayer and submitted to God and sensitive to His leadings (because anyone can hear from him) then when He gives direction and you execute it, it automatically makes it prophetic.

A person who operates in the prophetic is one who flows or is in the vein of the Ruach (Spirit) of God. One who is sensitive to the goings on in the realm of the Spirit and is used to demonstrating the power of the spoken word of God. They take heed by executing what is shown or heard from Holy Spirit. This is not the mantle of the Prophet, but just some qualities of the Prophet.

We will look at Dahveed's (David) anointing. He and Saul were both called by God to be king; however Dahveed's mantle gave him more authority to perform more duties. Saul was uncommitted to God, but still anointed. David was humble, repentant, and a worshiper of God. There is the kingly and then the priestly anointing. Praise and worship belonged to the priests. They were responsible for taking the people into the presence of God. The kingly anointing has a different weight to it. That is because it speaks of authority and dominion. We possess the kingly and priestly anointing, but we are usually in the priest's position praising God, worshiping the Father and not getting much further than that. What have we overtaken? David was a warrior - him and his mighty men. 1 Chronicles 11:10-26 David was a man of war. He subdued nations and he was honored and recognized for the battles that he won. 1 Chronicles 11:4-9 And he had a city named after him. (The city of David).

We have to walk in our kingly and priestly anointing; this is making full proof of our ministries (2 Timothy 4:5).

The Gifts

1 Corinthians 12:4-12

Now there are diversities of gifts, but the same Spirit. And there are differences of administrations, but the same Lord. And there are diversities of operations, but it is the same God which worketh all in all. But the manifestation of the Spirit is given to every man to profit withal. For to one is given by the Spirit the word of wisdom; to another the word of knowledge by the same Spirit; to another faith by the same Spirit; to another the gifts of healing by the same Spirit; to another the working of miracles; to another prophecy; to another discerning of spirits; to another divers kinds of tongues; to another the interpretation of tongues: but all these worketh that one and the selfsame Spirit, dividing to every man severally as He will. for as the body is one, and hath many members, and all the members of that one body, being many, are one body: so also is Christ.

Meditating on this portion of the scroll will keep us from comparing our gift to another person because we understand it is as the Spirit wills. Ruach Kodesh gives out the gifts, anointing, and so on and so forth. If you are found faithful in the small things, surely He will make you ruler over much. We do not have to be concerned with what someone else has or even what we have or think we don't have. There is nothing small about what He has given you. This is not a competition. It is a race. Just finish it.

WORSHIP

True Worship

Yeshua said those that worship, worship in spirit and in truth.

What is truth and what is worship?
Worship - 1. to honor or reverence as a divine being or supernatural power. 2. to regard with great or extravagant respect, honor, or devotion. Synonyms: adore, deify, glorify, revere, reverence, venerate.

The Hebrew word for worship is Shachah (pronounced- shah kah) it means to lie prostrate (flat) face to the ground in reverence and respect.

HEBREW WORDS FOR DANCE

There are many movements in the language of dance and we serve a God of movement. Hebrew is a verb oriented language which has a lot of movement involved. We go to the original language to get a dead on meaning of the word dance because English, a limited language, only has one word for dance. If you want to describe a particular type of dance you always have to add a word to it in order to know what type it is. You may want to do a study for yourself to go deeper. Jump on in.

Karar - to dance, whirl

Mechowlah - a dance company, dances, singing and dancing.

Exodus 15:20 KJV
Then Miriam the prophetess, the sister of Aaron, took the timbrel in her hand; and all the women went out after her with timbrels and with dances.

Mecholaw (plural) - dancing, specifically with singers and in a circle.

Jeremiah 31:4 KJV
Again I will build you, and you shall be rebuilt, O virgin of Israel. You shall again be adorned with your tambourines, And shall go forth in the dances of those who rejoice.

This is the same word Mechol (singular), Mecholaw (dance, dances, dancing).

2 Samuel 6:14 KJV
Then David danced before the Lord with all his might; and David was wearing a linen ephod.

This is the Hebrew whirl for dance called, karar. This means as he danced he whirled around. (I do a lot of that)

We know King David was an awesome worshiper and warrior before the Lord. Not only that, his worship in the dance was not alone. In the Israeli culture dance is a community matter. When the leader of a dance begins then something happens and the joy of the Lord is released and spread like a garment. The people joined in, they did not just stand around gazing.

In prophetic dance, or prophetic movement it is a bit different. Let me explain. The prophetic movement is the word of God in motion. It is a message to the people from the throne room.

It can be a word of direction, encouragement, correction, or an announcement. Even the praise is prophetic and it stretches out over the people (the garment of praise). As I stated earlier, in this ministry you minister out of your office and out of your sensitivity to Holy Spirits leading. As Yeshua's mother said to Him on the day He turned water into wine, *"Whatever He says to do, do it."* Yeshua, in the Book of John 2:1-11, had given a direction and the prophetic movement was for the men to fill the water pots with water and their obedience in doing it caused the miracle of wine to appear for the celebration of the wedding. This was Yeshua's first miracle. What will be yours?

1 Shmuel 18:6 (Samuel) KJV

And it came to pass as they came, when David was returned from the slaughter of the Philistine, that the women came out of all cities of Israel, singing and dancing, (v'hemechalot) to meet king Saul, with tabrets, with joy, and with instruments of music.

Again, this is the same word (it looks like one, but it is 2 words) this is plural because more than one person is dancing. We see the arsenal of singing, dancing, and tabrets with other instruments used here.

Arsenal is defined as a collection of weapons. We must understand that everything going on in the praise experience, Holy Spirit can at any time use the praise as a weapon against the enemy. There were banners (flags) flying here as well. It is a part of the celebration and banners where always used in war.

The banners were a sign of who it represented. Our banners represent Christ. Praise is a weapon. The devil hates to hear it. When we rise up and sing praises to the Lord, chains are loosed. Paul and Silas knew this when they found themselves in prison (Acts 16:5). At midnight they lifted their voices despite the situation and regardless of what it looked like. In the Bible, it has been recorded and states to send (Yehuda) Judah FIRST!"

Numbers 2:9 NIV

All the men assigned to the camp of Judah, according to their divisions, number 186,400. They will set out first.

Christ came from the tribe of Yehuda (Judah) and the Bible says He is preeminent and before all things, the head of the Church, and the firstborn from the dead (Colossians 1:18). *Yehuda (Judah) is the Hebrew word for praise. There is no "j" in Hebrew.

The Davidical Order

Dahveed (David) was a mighty warrior for Adonai, also known as the Master of legions (armies). He anointed and fashioned Dahveed for war and worship. Dahveed knew how to repent (turn) and worship (lie out before God in submission and adoration). He was skillful with his weapons whether it was a harp or a sling shot. Why? Because God was with him. David also was a king and a priest. Yes, these are two different mantles, and this was God's sovereign will that Dahveed move effectively in more than one area. He had various gifts and skills for various tasks given by the Lord, but we must remember it all began in the birth canal of intimacy. It is truly the secret place. He knew us before we were knitted in our mother's womb.

2 Samuel 6 KJV

And David danced before the LORD with all his might; and David was girded with a linen ephod. So David and all the house of Israel brought up the ark of the LORD with shouting, and with the sound of the trumpet. And as the ark of the LORD came into the city of David, Michal Saul's daughter looked through a window, and saw king David leaping and dancing before the LORD; and she despised him in her heart. And they brought in the ark of the LORD, and set it in his place, in the midst of the tabernacle that David had pitched for it: and David offered burnt offerings and peace offerings before the LORD.

2 Samuel 12:19 KJV

But when David saw that his servants whispered, he perceived that the child was dead. So he said to them, Is the child dead? And they said, He is. Then David arose from the floor, washed, anointed himself, changed his apparel, and went into the house of the Lord and worshiped. Then he came to his own house, and when he asked, they set food before him, and he ate.

Dahveed (David) worships regardless of what else is going on. In this passage his son dies because of a sin he committed with Bahtsheva (Bathsheba). Dahveed repented, fasted, got up and moved on in worship. This is the order and lifestyle of the followers of Christ. We have to get a handle on what is going on here. This is a life of total abandonment. This is leaving the way that "Church" does things and finding out from the wisdom of Holy Spirit on how things should be done according to the governmental and legislative mandates and protocol. As we read the Old Testament (Tankh/Hebrew Bible) we find that there was a certain way to enter into the tabernacle. Even in the natural to come into the presence of a king you had to know protocol. That seems to be a four lettered word these days with rogue people running around with the grace message and having no spiritual idea what it really means.

Esther, who was the king's beloved wife, could not just enter into his presence without being called. What a wonderful thing to know when we come into God's presence, He extends to us His Scepter of favor. Please note that not only is there a double edged sword, but there is another side to the scepter as well. David knew what side of the scepter he was on. He understood and made sure everyone else understood what side they were on, what they should be doing, and how they should do it. Our problem is that we don't bother to learn and we don't ask Ruach Kodesh to teach us. David fought with what he was intimate with. He could not wear Saul's armor and he could not make it fit. This man knew about God and because of his sincere intimacy, he knew what fit in worship. He understood the strings and when to bring them in and he knew how many singers to bring in to make Gods praise glorious. He had so many because he was amplifying the sound that he heard from heaven and from his lone days in the hills watching over the sheep. He understood the heart of the shepherd because he was one. He understood the heart of God and found a place there. He hated what God hated. Sure, he messed up. Don't we all fall and stumble before we learn to walk? Don't we long after things that we know we should not have? Of course we do. We must come to a place where we decide if we are on the Lord's side or on the side of His enemies. Crossing the line on either side is a prophetic movement because everything we do has consequences in the realm of the spirit and are governed by laws whether we know what those laws are or not. Find out the protocol of the Spirit and then you will make your ways prosperous.

Part of this relationship with God is allowing Ruach Kodesh to clean us from the inside out. We are so busy wanting to look good on the outside, but He is coming back for a church without spot or wrinkle. Most serious spots or stains are on the inside of us. Remember Yeshua said it is those things on the inside that defile us. We cannot be effective in ministry without being clean on the inside. Tell Holy Spirit that you want to be clean from the inside. Remember on television years ago they would say, "This is a job for superman!" Well, this walk with Christ is a job for Holy Spirit.

Lord, clean my mind and my heart. Make me new and cause me to realize that I am new. Close the door to the old and take away the reproach. Bring me to a place of humility and be my gate keeper. Cause me to be sensitive to Your Spirit. Don't let the enemy triumph over me. Cause me to walk in Your righteous ways and give me shalom. Show me how to really trust you. Amen.

The King of kings (Melech HaMelechim)

Matthew 2:11 KJV

And on going into the house, they saw the Child with Mary His mother, and they fell down and worshiped Him. Then opening their treasure bags, they presented to Him gifts--gold and frankincense and myrrh.

He is the Way, the Truth, and the Life. When we worship Him, we give it all to Him. We pour our praise, everything we have, and all that we are on Him like oil. We are to be a sweet smelling fragrance in His nostrils. In worship, we become a fragrant bouquet for Him to admire and take in. He should be able to look down and smile on that which He created, called, and chose. He should see humility, brokenness, and total submission. We want to be sold out. Let's look at some words for worship.

Shachah- this means to lie prostrate in worship - to depress or prostrate in homage or loyalty to God, bow down, fall down flat.

Psalm 29:2 KJV
Give unto the Lord the glory due to his name; Worship the Lord in the beauty of holiness.

In this culture, we think worship is standing on our feet and lifting our hands. That is not how worship is described in the Bible. It is always described as falling to one's knees or lying down on one's face. Let's give God His due. I mean think about it. Can you really stand in His Presence?

This is what I call the floor or carpet ministry. Laying stretched out in His presence is indicative of you laying at His glorious feet.

Barak - to kneel or bow, to give reverence to God as an act of adoration, implies a continual conscious giving place to God, to be in tune to Him and His presence.

How can you demonstrate this in a dance? What song best works? What does He want from you? There are many songs that could be used to fall down and lie prostrate. It could be done at the end of the song. If you have a few extra vessels to use, some of them can fall down in Shachah. Shekinah Glory has a song called, "All hail the king." It is a song one of many where one can take 20 seconds to lay out. There is another song by, Bishop Paul Morton called, "Bow Down and Worship Him" and it may be an old song, but it works. Alberto and Kimberly Rivera have music known as prophetic music or soaking sessions (www.rainingpresence.com). I have their expressed permission to minister their songs. It is always best to get the permission of the artists. Some of them would prefer it.

Psalm 95:6 KJV

Oh come, let us worship and bow down; Let us kneel before the Lord our maker.

Guwl - to spin around, under the influence of any violent emotion Psalm 32:11 Be glad in the Lord and rejoice, you righteous; And shout for joy, all you upright in heart.

Ranan - to creak, to emit a stridulous (making a shrill creaking sound), to shout aloud for joy

Psalm 98:4 KJV

Shout joyfully to the Lord, all the earth; Break forth in song, rejoice, and sing praises.

Shuwr - strolling minstrelsy, to sing, singer (man or woman)

Psalm 18:49 KJV

Therefore I will give thanks to you, O Lord, among the Gentiles, and sing praises to your name.

Psalm 33:3 KJV

Sing to him a new song; Play skillfully with a shout of joy

Tehillah - to sing hallal, a new song, a hymn of spontaneous praise glorifying God in song

Psalm 34:1 KJV
I will bless the Lord at all times; His praise shall continually be in my mouth.

(Note: Sometimes the Lord will have you prophesy to someone in song.) This also can be incorporated in your prophetic dance piece.

Todah - an extension of the hand, avowal, adoration, a choir of worshipers, confession, sacrifice of praise, thanksgiving

Psalm 50:14 KJV
Offer to God thanksgiving, and pay your vows to the Most High.

This word "todah" also means, "Thank you"

Zamar - to touch the strings or parts of a musical instrument i.e. play upon it, to make music accompanied by the voice, to celebrate in song and music, give praise, sing forth praises, psalms

Psalm 66:2 KJV
Sing out the honor of his name; Make his praise glorious.

Psalm 71:22 KJV
I will also praise You with the harp, even Your truth and faithfulness, O my God; unto You will I sing praises with the lyre, O Holy One of Israel.

COLORS

Biblically, colors do hold meaning. This is another aspect or language of God. What He chooses to say is up to Him. If He can speak through a mule, then He can use colors. As a color is worn or waved, it is moving through the atmosphere causing a shift and a transformation. Let us lean not to our own understanding, but lean on the wisdom of Holy Spirit.

I encourage you to study the colors you use. Let the Lord choose the colors for you because it is His message you are bringing, not your own. I personally do not like to see anyone ministering in the color black. By wearing black, what are you saying? What is God saying? If He has given you a piece to do and that color is on you or someone to represent some dark spirit or situation then it is fine. However, if you are dancing about the glory of God, His faithfulness, or any good thing, then no, you should not be in this color.

Black represents sin, depression, dark thoughts, evil etc. I will say this; God is sovereign and He can do and use whatever He likes at any time because He knows all things and we do not.

In addition, when you are ministering keep your mind set on Him, not who is watching you. God should be seen. Are you coming in His Name or your own? This is not so much a how to book as it is a Who to manual. Our heart beat is unto Elohim and then it pours out to the people. We must be filled with Him before we can do anything else. We need to have that eye to eye closeness and this would include intimate moments with Him. I recall when I first started out in this ministry I was so nervous (still am) and I always looked up as I moved around the room. I always kept my focus on Him. We cannot shrink back and be afraid of the faces of people. In order to find our strength we must delight ourselves in Him.

What is really important is our love walk. Study 1 Corinthians 13 to see what love really is. We cannot say we love God and have disdain for our brothers or sisters who we see every day. Love is not jealous, puffed up, or envious. It has patience and is kind. Love has hope for all things. God is love and Yeshua is our example of love. How dare we take communion when we have ill will towards someone? Who cares if they don't like you or talk about you? They talked about Yeshua. Why not you too? We have to get over it. No one has ever done to you what they did to Him. Your trial is not greater than His so we have to learn not to be offended and learn to love, it is His commandment. Loving God and loving people are the two commandments which pleases the King of Glory. We cannot get pass this. Remember when Yeshua told the story? Lord, Lord we prophesied in Your Name, we cast out demons; we did this and that in Your Name. We danced for you. His reply was, "Really? I never knew you." I am paraphrasing, but look at the Scripture and let Holy Spirit speak to your heart. You know when you are out of order when you look in the Book of Truth.

Mattayahu 7:21- 23 (Matthew) KJV

Not everyone that saith unto me, Lord, Lord, shall enter into the kingdom of Heaven; but he that doeth the will of my Father which is in Heaven. Many will say to me in that day, Lord, Lord, have we not prophesied in thy name? and in thy name have cast out devils? and in thy name done many wonderful works? And then will I profess unto them, I never knew you: depart from me, ye that work iniquity.

Wow, He will tell it to our faces. Full frontal confrontation causes us to know without a shadow of a doubt when we are out of order. My God, we have to get it right. Many want to be in ministry, but what are their motives? If we really look at this text He is talking about Christians, not unbelievers. They said, "Lord, Lord." What a shame to be in ministry and think that you have been in a good place just to find out after it was all over, that you were not.

Let's get it right before we get left. We must delight ourselves in Him and Ruach Kodesh will always give us truth, not just about Him, but about ourselves. We must walk the narrow path. We cannot be like, look like, live like, or minister like others. We are to imitate Christ alone. We cannot covet anything, but spiritual gifts. We cannot covet someone else's gift, but the gifts of Ruach Kodesh.

1 Corinthians 12:31 KJV
Now concerning spiritual gifts, brethren, I would not have you ignorant.

1 Corinthian 12:7 CJB ... Let us look closer at this text.
Moreover, to each person is given the particular manifestation of the Spirit that will be for the common good.

This is what we must remember: each person is given a particular manifestation of the Spirit. Your portion is to use it for the common good. It is the portion Ruach has given to you to use as He wills, how He wills, and for whom He wills. We must submit to His program. We do want Him to be pleased with our praise, but mostly with our lifestyles. We don't want to be anointed only when we put on our garments to minister. We don't want to just have those high moments in front of the communities (congregations). We want a consecrated life before the King of kings. Besides, if our lifestyles are not where they should be you won't be before the community holding that position for long. He is after a Bride and a church without spot or wrinkle. He is calling us higher and closer.

With all our flags, banners, timbrels, and whatever else He has given us as tools of praise and evangelism, (some call them props- I don't like that term) let us not forsake time with Him and the eating of His holy scroll, the whole scroll. Ruach Kodesh says we should invest in ourselves. Don't look at garments, banners, and flags as being too expensive. You are an expensive and fragrant aroma. You should have the best, and believe me, if it is for you, He will see that you get it. I cannot tell you all the times someone sowed into me. However, I still needed to sow into my own ministry. I had to know my own value. Eating the scroll of Proverbs 31:10-31 is such a bracha (blessing). When you look at it in Ivreet (Hebrew), you will see that every verse is in alphabetical order. Ruach Kodesh was saying that this woman had an excellent character and not only that, there is an order to getting to a place of balance, joy, peace, and fruitfulness.

DANCE IS A LANGUAGE

We are not familiar with symbols like ת ר ו ה and why not? I will tell you why. It is because we have not been taught. We did not even bother to learn and realize that these "symbols" are our way of living, these symbols when we put them together spell Torah in Hebrew it does not mean law as some would say, but it means instruction, journey, to teach. This is as true for prophetic movement as it is for the Hebrew language. Dance is another language much like Hebrew, because Hebrew is a verb oriented language. It is about movement and function. It is not stagnant and it is geared to draw you closer to the source as you read, write, and speak it. The more we understand our function, the more effective we will be. We have to lend ourselves to the lesson that is our journey. This includes our ministry and please make a note that just as we stretch our minds to learn, it is the same as we stretch our bodies. As we move and strengthen them in the spirit and natural, it gains a wider and deeper vocabulary. I call it thoughts from the throne. We must invest our time and attention to the gifts in us as faithful (secure/firm) stewards. Prayer and communication with the Father is the prime investment, for without Him we can do nothing (John 15). This is the first investment as is eating the scroll of Elohim. Ruach Kodesh wants to teach you all things.

Listen for the Voice of the Lord in your ministry. Don't be like the five foolish virgins who were caught without oil. Truly, I tell you to go out without the anointing, understanding, and hearing is as a high speed train about to derail. Take His yoke and learn FROM Him. Truly, it is easy. Shalom

PROPHETIC MOVEMENT

Psalm 139 Complete Jewish Bible:

ADONAI, you have probed me, and you know me. You know when I sit and when I stand up, you discern my inclinations from afar, you scrutinize my daily activities. You are so familiar with all my ways that before I speak even a word, ADONAI, you know all about it already. You have hemmed me in both behind and in front and laid your hand on me. Such wonderful knowledge is beyond me, far too high for me to reach. Where can I go to escape your Spirit? Where can I flee from your presence? If I climb up to heaven, you are there; if I lie down in Sh'ol, you are there. If I fly away with the wings of the dawn and land beyond the sea, even there your hand would lead me, your right hand would hold me fast. If I say, "Let darkness surround me, let the light around me be night," even darkness like this is not too dark for you; rather, night is as clear as day, darkness and light are the same. For you fashioned my inmost being, you knit me together in my mother's womb. I thank you because I am awesomely made, wonderfully; your works are wonders -I know this very well. My bones were not hidden from you when I was being made in secret, intricately woven in the depths of the earth. Your eyes could see me as an embryo, but in your book all my days were already written; my days had been shaped before any of them existed. God, how I prize your thoughts! How many of them there are! If I count them, there are more than grains of sand; if I finish the count, I am still with you. God, if only you would kill off the wicked! Men of blood, get away from me! They invoke your name for their crafty schemes; yes, your enemies misuse it. ADONAI, how I hate those who hate you! I feel such disgust with those who defy you! I hate them with unlimited hatred! They have become my enemies too. Examine me, God, and know my heart; test me, and know my thoughts. See if there is in me any hurtful way, and lead me along the eternal way

Earlier I gave scriptural reference to prophetic movement. Here are some of my experiences in prophetic movements in dance.

I was in Covington, Ga, in 2008 and was asked to minister by the Pastor. It was interesting because Holy Spirit sent me there and told me towards the end of the service that the Pastor was going to ask me to minister in dance. With my crazy self I responded, "But she does not even know me." Why do we do these things as if the Lord does not know what He is talking about? Anyway, I saw a friend of mine who I worked with at school and she also ministered in dance. I was wondering what she was doing there, but I recognized one of her garments on someone so I figured she had her young dancers there to minister. Now, mind you, I had never been to this church before, or so I thought. I mean nothing there was familiar to me, but we will get back to that.

The girls ministered and I thought to myself that this is why Ruach Kodesh told me to come there so I could see them. This is called, assumption. When service was over I was trying to get out of there ASAP. It was a great service, but I was trying to leave because I was never a person to hang around after service. My friend saw me and asked what I was doing there, it was her mother's church. I was stunned. She did not mean her mom was a member. She meant that her mom was the Pastor. Wow, I was feeling set up! We had five seconds of small talk, but I tried to make my way out and she said, "Wait, I want to introduce you to my mom!" I said ok to her and she took my hand and led me through the crowd. She says, "Mom, this is the Prophetess who dances that I told you about." Her mother looked at me and smiled and said, "Amen, it is so nice to meet you...." And here it came. She asked the question, "....can you minister for us tonight? We have a revival."

Ruach Kodesh told me and here it was in my face in the same hour. "Sure, it would be my pleasure." They gave me the details about the time and such and I was back there that evening and prayed up. Ruach Kodesh showed me what to do. I do not ever rehearse or practice. Holy Spirit (Ruach Kodesh) gives me the song and the garment and I go in worship mode with my ears attentive to direction.

While we were all praying I was shown in the Spirit to wear my purple dress. I had two dresses one was purple and the other was white. Then Holy Spirit gave me a vision of me wrapping someone up in my purple dress. This is how I knew which one to wear. I did not have enough fabric on the other dress to do it. It pays to be obedient. The purple dress was long and wide. By the time I got out there to minister, I had forgotten the vision. You can actually see this video on my YouTube channel under Take the Limits Off by Israel and New Breed.

It was a prophetic movement when I wrapped this women in my dress and she collapsed under the power of God. The other prophetic movement was when I shook my dress out later on in this same video. I had never seen or heard of such things as wrapping someone up in my dress. Recently, with a flag I made, the Lord had me wrap a young man up in it. That is how big my flag is. I had never heard of this either, but the power of God was present. I thought I was done and was about to go to my room, but as I passed him the Lord had me back up and go minister to him.

These are not things that you see someone do and you copy. The counterfeit/copycat spirit is not approved by God! If He shows it to you then you go forth in it. This was a part of my field training and it really tested my obedience. I had never been to a dance conference or a workshop or anything like that at that time. When I say He was my mentor and trainer, I mean it.

Now, I said I would get back to the church I thought I had never been to. Apparently, I had been there once. I was at my church and ministered in dance and was to be baptized (again) after service with some others. I was so drunk after ministering they had to help me to get to that church and it had a pool for us. They helped me in and out of the water. I had been drunk in the spirit for so long! I think it was a couple of hours. I recall being baptized barely. That Yeshua is so funny! He sends me there to minister months and months later. I did not recognize the place at all.

The Scripture for shaking out my garment is found in **Nehemiah 5:13 NIV**. I had never seen this scripture before I did that and only saw it quite recently.

I also shook out the folds of my robe and said, "In this way may God shake out of his house and possessions every man who does not keep this promise. So may such a man be shaken out and emptied!" At this the whole assembly said, "Amen," and praised the LORD. And the people did as they had promised.

Prophetic movement

We have to begin to understand the mind of God and His language. For those of you who dream, Ruach Kodesh desires for you to understand the message that has been downloaded into you. The message may be personal about you, your destiny, character, etc. It may be about the body of Christ, the government, your family, boss, neighbor, leadership, or just about anything or anyone. Understand that when it comes from the Lord, it is prophetic in nature. It is a movement because it is in the Spirit. The dove is a representation of the Spirit of God - it flies. Water represents the Spirit of God - it flows. The blood of Christ flows through every area of our lives and the word tells us that life is in the blood.

Leviticus 17:11 GWT
Because blood contains life, I have given this blood to you to make peace with me on the altar. Blood is needed to make peace with me.

The next thing I want to share is that we must understand the the Bible which was originally written in Hebrew is a picture book. It tells stories and all the stories start out with symbols. We understand symbols. When we see a picture of a tree it does not say the word tree, but we know what it is. We recognize symbols as numbers and letters and strung together we can generally make sense of it. As we drive down the road we see signs and it tells us what direction we ought to go in or they may give us warnings and things of that nature.

Deuteronomy 11:8 HNV says, *therefore shall you lay up My words in your heart and in your soul; and you shall bind them for a sign on your hand, and they shall be for symbols between your eyes.*

Some translations use the word frontlets. This consists of a leather band worn on the forehead and has some of the scriptures from Exodus 13 and Deuteronomy 6:4 which are known as the sacred shma or shemah. Hear O Yisrael the Lord is One.

The eagle is the symbol of the prophetic. We do understand these things and yet there are many things we don't yet understand. Yeshua told His talmidim (disciples) that there was much He wanted to tell them, but it would be too much for them (John 16:12).

The Hebrew letters are symbols and they not only speak, but have life because they move. Hebrew is a verb oriented language and is concrete which means there is no ambiguity. Once you learn them then you know them. Each letter has prophetic properties and each letter speaks. For instance the fifth letter of the Hebrew alef bet is hey. It represents grace and it means behold, as in look!

I am not giving Hebrew lessons in this book. I do teach Hebrew, but for the purposes of the prophetic movement I have to bring it up. God wants us to understand the mind of Christ and we must realize that Christ was a Jewish Rabbi. He taught as one with authority. The Jews then and now teach and when they do, they always reference Master Scribes or Rabbi's such as Rashi. They do not usually mention themselves, they always mention what Rashi said or thought on a particular subject. In Biblical times, they always referenced the Law of Moshe' and so when Yeshua spoke with the type of weight that His mantle carried, they were cut to the heart and astounded.

This is the art of prophetic movement. It is weighty and authoritative. No one could or can refute the wisdom of God. Some may not like it, but it is what it is. That should settle it.

We have to bring our minds up to His level and not dumb Him down to ours. He came through a Jewish lineage; He is the Lion of the Tribe of Yehuda (Judah). Hebrew (Ivreet) is what Abram was called in the Torah. In Genesis (Bereshit) 14:13, One who had escaped, came and reported this to Abram the Hebrew. Abraham had a grandson named Eber from the word Abar meaning one from the other side. This is interesting that Yeshua came down from the other side into this side the earth realm. Hebrew letters are written from the other side which is right to left. My point in this is that there may be many people who do not know this side of the prophetic, but it is time they embraced it because it is the way of the Lord. We have to get on that way (path). He speaks wonderful things, but it is up to us to accept all He says. We cannot lean to our own understanding, Proverbs (Mishlei) 3:5.

Eloheinu (Our God) is The Authority. Remember His mother Miriam (Mary) said, *"whatever He tells you to do, do it."* Did it look silly pouring water into wine jugs and expecting wine? I am sure it did. I can imagine someone yelling, "We are out of wine! What will we do?" and here you come telling folks, "Pour some water in to those jars over there." If they are obedient, there is your prophetic movement and there shall be a performance! There shall be increase and manifestation! But we have to SUPPORT and align ourselves with His word. Without it, what we say is dead and has no life in it.

The Garments speak. What are you saying when your feet hit the floor? Did you pick out the garment or did Holy Spirit? Some think it does not matter. I beg to differ. All of my garments are chosen by the Lord. They are priestly garments because I have a ministry of prophetic intercession. If you call me to minister, then by virtue of my mantle, my garment, and weapons of choice I come with an assignment to shift, break, tear down, destroy and then usher the Presence of the Almighty in the place and into the set of people in attendance. This is not because of me. I am no one. My identity is in Christ alone. I do not testify of myself, but I let my works testify of Him Who sent me. This is the way it should be no matter how stunning one thinks my garments are. They represent the Kingdom and there is nothing drab about it. I am not saying that something simple as a linen garment is not of the Kingdom. On the contrary, it is very scriptural. And again, He is sovereign and He can use whatever He likes. This is after all an audience of One.

The Shofar speaks. It has various sounds that are quite distinct to the trained ear. The problem is that many are in an untrained army. In scripture when you see the word trumpet it refers to the shofar or the ram's horn. Different sounds mean different things.

1 Corinthians 14:8 NIV

Again, if the trumpet does not sound a clear call, who will get ready for battle?

Joel 2:1 KJV
Blow ye the trumpet in Zion, and sound an alarm in my holy mountain: let all the inhabitants of the land tremble: for the day of the LORD cometh, for it is nigh at hand.

Revelations 10:7 KJV
But in the days when the seventh angel is about to sound his trumpet, the mystery of God will be accomplished, just as he announced to his servants the prophets.

Matthew 6:2 NIV
So when you give to the needy, do not announce it with trumpets, as the hypocrites do in the synagogues and on the streets, to be honored by men. I tell you the truth, they have received their reward in full.

The sounds are:
Teruah - 9 short quick blasts. This is like an alarm clock. Wake up! Be alert!
Tekia- 1 long straight blast- This is done on Rosh Hashanah.
When one hears it they know it is our Kings' coronation
Shevarim- 3 medium wailing sounds. This is like a cry. Think of a little kid crying and they have that stutter/stop/start sound in their cry.

The shofar goes through a rigorous process after being cut from the kudu antelope (from Africa) it has an awful stench, it has to be dug out and then there is a drilling process to purify its sound. After that, there is heat added to soften it and to straighten out the part that leads to the mouth piece. It is quite interesting how there is heat and pressure added to turn the shofar in the direction of the one who has it in his hands and then it is pressed against the grinding wheel to remove the rough exterior as to expose the beauty underneath. Finally, it is given a nice polish. The curve is a reminder of man bending his will to the will of the Lord. Doesn't that sound familiar? No pun intended!

We go through this same process. We are first cut away from our old life and given a new purpose. Then begins the digging, the grinding, the breath of God being placed in us so that we have a pure sound. He turns our hearts in His direction and onto His paths. The old is removed and the beauty from within is exposed for all to see. A beautiful vessel.

There is a sound we make to the people that calls them to repentance, Teshuvah, which literally means to turn and get back where you were before you got lost. Then there is a sound we make to alert others to assemble for war or assemble for a corporate fast. There is yet another sound of rejoicing and celebration. Yes, we are so like the shofar in the Masters hands.

The process of death to life—
From being formed and deformed by sin.
Reformed by the work of Christ and
finally transformed by Ruach Kodesh.
We die, but yet live.
We dance and now do sing.
We bow and do lie before Him
How Great is our God.

In quantum physics, there is a term calling popping a qwiff. We have to pop Gods qwiff! Let me explain. In quantum physics there is something that the naked eye cannot see, but it is there waiting to be seen and it is only then that it becomes active. This quantum wave collapse, caused by observation, is called popping a qwiff. There is so much we do not understand. I don't want to go all science on you. I am no scientist, but there are things that occur in the unseen realm that science really can explain. For example we heard the term traveling faster than the speed of light. Well, in order for the word of God to get to us in a vision or when He deposits it into our spirits it has to travel faster than the speed of light. He is showing us something not yet realized in this dimension from another dimension. He wants us to take that word or action and run with it so men can "see" it. This is Him telling us to write the vision out and make it plain. In other words, make it visible what He has shown us so others can now see it and manifest it in THIS realm. Everything we behold with our eyes has come from the mind's eye first. It can come from your holy imagination or unholy imagination which is of the enemy. Just look around you. This book in your hand was just an idea in my mind planted by Holy Spirit. A garment, a chair, a stereo, laser cd, a stove, etc. Someone had to perceive it in their heart and mind and say, "I am going to create or make this thing that I have seen." This is why we see some of those testimonies that people walk around with manifest. It is because what God has shown them (and this has been my experience) has come to pass because they saw it, supported it, and aligned themselves to receive it. Hello!!

Prophetic movement is a mandate from Heaven. When a movement is being displayed it should serve as a sign to the people that such and such is going to happen or be released or torn down, etc. However, the people have to catch it in the spirit to discern it. Yeshua told Johns' disciples "Tell him that the deaf are hearing, the blind are seeing, and the dead are being raised." This sign was an answer to the question, "How will we know who the Messiah is?" Miracles signs and wonders will follow them that believe. In Jewish culture, when they asked for a sign it was because God always said to them if they were unsure about something. *"And this will be a sign to you..."* Luke 2:12 concerning the birth of Christ. Exodus 12:13 speaks to us that the sign was the blood on the door post. 2 Kings 19:29 was a sign to Hezekiah.

We have to start believing (supporting) the Vision of God and the visions He is giving us. This sefer (book) is for those who want to get on the road to Damascus and have the same experience of hearing the Lord correct us, show us how blind we were in what we thought we were doing, and then send someone to restore us with the right vision.

Prophetic Dance is different than that of a regular praise dance although at times it can be prophetic. Prophetic dance is the word of the Lord in action. One prophecies by what they do with their hands and with various movements. It is the Ruach Kodesh moving the vessel or vessels to move in a way in which the Lord Himself directs. One can shift the atmosphere by virtue of a particular move or movements of his or her body, or by the waving of a flag or anything else the Lord desires to use. He may send you to a person or a group of people at a particular part of a song because it is for them personally. It is the stomping, shaking, twirling, running, waving, singing, standing, warring, travailing, shouting, praising, or anything that is coming directly from Him for you to execute. You may be guided to use ribbons, banners, a staff, and scarves. It is He

chooses to lead you. This is where the anointing is. Without it, it's just a nice dance piece. We want to break the chains that have people bound. We want to remove the yokes and remove all the waste places in their lives, not entertain them.

Prophetic dance is for the edification of a person or a people. It is the expressed heart of The Father to His beloved. It is a rhema word in motion. The Bible is a picture book, you can dance the word from Berehsheet (Genesis) to Revelation.

Anything that comes out of the mouth of the Father is prophetic. With just one word He can change our lives. His Name is the Bread of Life.

1 Thessalonians 5:19-20 AMP
Do not quench (suppress or subdue) the [Holy] Spirit; do not spurn the gifts and utterances of the prophets [do not depreciate prophetic revelations nor despise inspired instruction or exhortation or warning

kingdom songs vs secular songs

You thought I forgot? Please understand these two things. Psalm 33:3 CJB says, *Sing to him a new song; play skillfully, and shout for joy.*

This should tell us there are enough kingdom songs in the Spirit that we can draw from and Tehillim (Psalm) 40:3 says, *"He has given me a new song to sing, a hymn of praise to our God."* Many will see what he has done and be amazed. They will put their trust in the LORD.

We can trust in the Lord to always supply the NEW! We do not want to be reminded of the old things because He says that they are done

away with. We thing eight means new beginnings, but in fact it means to put off. It is the old man that we must put off and it is only then that we experience the newness of the life that Christ offers us. Now we know He is sovereign and can do whatever He likes, but trust that He will give you what to say, sing, and minister to the lost, to encourage the broken, and reconcile those who have gone out of His pasture. As the Psalm said, "Many will see what He has done and be amazed. They will put their trust in the Lord."

EXERCISES

Here are some exercises you can do to get closer to God, gain a better understanding, and learn to move according to His word.

1. Defining

Learn to breathe. Take deep breaths and try to relax yourself. Defining is a time to search out who you are. Are you a warrior, intercessor, Prophet, prophetic, one who weeps between the porch and the altar, burden bearer, seer, peace bringer, etc? We should be all these things, really. What you want to do is have those moments with Him to find out who you really are. Let Him define you and show you your parameter and how wide your spiritual circumference is. When I moved sometimes I had to stand in a room and move as if I had a hammer in my hand and knocked out one brick at a time. I moved in a circle as if I was hemmed in, and I broke out. This was a defining moment for me. I was spiritually released from what others thought I was and who I thought I was. The limitations that people put on me had to come off. We serve a limitless God. See if you can with your vision extend the boarders and see a bit further.

2. Listening

Listening means that you are no longer talking. We tend to do the monologue instead of the dialogue. Learn and study to be quite. Take a few minutes to sit and wait for Him to say something. You can ask the Lord, "Give me this day my daily bread. What is the word or the direction for me today, Lord? You said if I acknowledge you in all my ways that You would direct my path. We have so many things going on that our minds get busy and sometimes is on auto pilot. We have to have a shutdown mode in His Presence. We must be able to hear Him, especially in the midst of chaos.

3. Movement

You can start by playing worship music and have what I refer to as soaking sessions for a few minutes a day with your note pad and pen ready to write down what He says to you or shows you. Please have your Bible as well because you may want to start out reading a passage on worship as in one of the Psalms, but do not rely on this alone. He may have you, as stated in Psalm 100, to enter into His Presence with singing. Sing to Him something you already know or sing a new song. Soon a dance, a move, a wave of the arms will begin. It may be a twirl...just flow with it. Zephaniah 3:17 says that the Lord sings over us. Don't you think He would expect a response from within you?

4. Reflective Time

Silence helps us to hear God. Sit in silence for one full minute and empty out the cares of the day and all of the things that would distract you. Can you sit in silence and think on God without other things crowding your thoughts and vying for your attention? Can you give Him one minute without asking Him anything? Then two full minutes. Every day for one week. One minute when you wake up and one minute before you go to sleep. The following week try for two minutes. No music, no added anything. You are giving up your mind to Him. Find a scripture to meditate on. Then give it your FULL attention. Wait for Him to speak to you. He may or He may not speak. This exercise is for you, not Him. This will help you to grow in your hearing. We cannot minister to Him if we cannot hear from Him.

You should always have a journal with you and one near your bed. You never know when the Lord is going to speak to you and if He gives you a dream write it down. You may not understand it, but write it down anyway. This shows you are: 1. Respectful of what He wants to say; 2. In great expectation of what He wants to say to you; 3. You understand He can speak at any time. 4. You want to be ready.

5. **Define the following words: Then eat it.**

Intimacy
Enjoin
Posture
Herald
Communicate
Hear
Travail
Demolish
Prophecy
Engage

Look these words up. I will not give you the definition because you are the one who has to draw near to Him and then He will draw nearer to you. This is about relationship and how dearly you want to be closer to Him and hear His voice. As I stated earlier, this is more than "dancing." Anyone can dance, but you want to minister in it and move prophetically. You need the anointing that breaks yokes and burdens. You want to be unique in what you do and it all must be to His glory. Humility is the beginning of your journey. The journey is Torah. This is Orchayim (Way of Life). Torah is like a Father standing behind his child pointing in the direction they should go. The father always knows the way because he has traveled it and seen it. We must learn to listen to the voice of Wisdom and trust that there is a prescribed path for all of us and in different seasons.

Matthew 6:33 KJV

Seek ye FIRST the Kingdom of God and His righteousness and all these things will be added to you.

A prayer you say...

Father, make me to know you in a greater way, break everything off and out of me that will hinder me from getting to the destined place. Call me out of the mediocre and set my feet in the greater. I want to walk humbly before You. Teach me. Teach me everything I need to know via Holy Spirit. Robe me in Your righteousness and put Your ring on my finger. Make me to know wisdom and courage. Take away every false image. Cause me to align myself with the identity You gave me. You desire truth in my inward parts. According to Psalm 5, Holy Spirit minister to me about love and giving. Pull me out of the arena of entertainment, compromise, comparison, and competition. Create in me a clean heart and renew the righteous spirit within me. I want to rest in You and not stagger at Your precious and great promises. Cause me to be still in Your presence and move only by Your Spirit. I decree that no spirit will rule over me and that You, Lord are my gate keeper. I walk away from sin and the influence of others. Bring those around me that You have destined for me. Teach me to hear and heed to Your wise counsel. I want to know You and be found faithful. Amen.

ABOUT THE AUTHOR

Nabiyah Baht Yehuda (Prophet of God, daughter of praise in Hebrew) is a member of Voices of Christ Literary Ministry International and a Master Scribe. Prophet Nabiyah is a master scribe trained and certified at the Prophetic School Of The Scribe by Apostle Theresa Johnson, Founder of The Voices of Christ Literary Ministries International. She is the Founder of The Chamber Room Experience and the Executive Director of For His Glory Prophetic Movement Dance Ministry. Nabiyah has had a love for dance since she was a young girl in NYC. She trained as an actress at the Billie Holiday Theater in Brooklyn, N.Y. She is a spoken word artist and has written many inspirational songs and poetry. Nabiyah also teaches the Bible with a Hebrew/Jewish mindset. Holy Spirit led her to begin this journey of learning Hebrew in 2004. She has done spoken word in churches and on the open mic circuit always glorifying Her

Savior. She also has done a few Christian plays in and around Georgia and New York City.

Her resurrection into Christ was August 22, 1998 in Brooklyn NY. Eight months after she was saved, she would dance before the Lord in her bedroom not knowing one day He would allow her to minister in prophetic movement before His congregations. She was and continues to be taught of the Lord and loves to share that gift with others. She ministers prophetically in worship and praise dances at different ministries, schools, and hospitals or where ever the Lord calls for her to go. Her motto is, "It's not just dance; it's the Word in motion." Everything that she knows about dance and worship she has learned via Holy Spirit.

She works with men and women of all ages teaching not just dance, but worship. "If I can reach out into the audience and usher them into my worship experience and a prophetic movement then maybe they can feel God at work in their lives." We overcome the devil by the blood of the lamb and the word of our testimonies. She is at the time of writing this book, attending seminary for her degree of Masters of Divinity.

She recognizes that the Lord has been gracious to her and is honored that He has given her such a beautiful gift to be able to show forth His word in motion. She has come to understand His hand in the worship arts and He has given her a love for it and a desire to teach it. Her prayer is that the Church receive this manifestation of the gift of Ruach Kodesh as another vehicle of love to usher the people of God and all creation into His most glorious presence. Shalom Alechem (peace unto you).

For events, teaching, and updates, visit:

www.thoughtsfromthethrone.vpweb.com

www.youtube.com/forhisgloryga

www.bhncollege.com

www.reclaimingyourvoice.org

Prophetic Movement can be the fluid motion of your body in dance, but it can also be your pen moving to the inspirational voice of Ruach Kodesh.

Here is my Poetic Prophetic Movement...

Lover of my soul

You have called-do I dare answer
You have breathed my name.
Abba, how can I not answer.
You have spinned me out with Your own
Hand. You anointed me with Your oil and I
bring it back to Your Feet.
You have sang sweet songs of deliverance over me.
And I dance-I dance.
May I have this dance?
My King I do bow
Before You I cry aloud.
These tears that spill down are not sadness
But it springs from sweet joy found.
Spinning wildly with banner in hand-yes
His banner over me is ahava-love.
Yes-You have called.
Yes-You have breathed my name.
How can I NOT answer?
This Love I cannot contain.
Precious is this oil I've found
I want to praise You with all that is within me.
I am no longer bound.
Freedom is my dance.
Love is in my spin.

Take me from my past-my past.
My own hand points to my future.
You guide me with Your Eye.
The fire in me won't relent so
Why should I?
I chase after You with my praise.
I reach out to You- I wanna see Your Face.
Your grace in me surrounds me like a shield and Your
banner over me is Love.
I wave a white flag of surrender.
I do surrender.

Adonai Oh, Majestic One

He who sits high and looks low
Hear me in the night season and visit with me
Capture my heart and do what You will.

Pierce thru the dark places in me O, Lord!
Remove from me the vain things
Purge me Abba, Tahare, Tahare (cleanse)
Like silver, like gold...isn't it just like you? Not Yet...

Call to Yourself the precious parts of Yourself in me
Show me the image that You called me to be
I am purchased and lo, I am not my own
Cause me to recall that this is flesh on bone.

Precious is the death of Your saints in Your eyes
Precious is Your sanctified ones who seek to die
Promises You gave to those who would follow
Never turning back; pursing towards tomorrow

Where Your hands have called
Destiny is sure
Woe unto me
I can endure no more...flesh trying to live.

No more flesh Just
bring to me death
so that my spirit can live; my spirit can live, my spirit will
live, my...spirit...lives

That I may do Your will...
Fulfill your will, purpose in my heart Your will... incorruptible
seed in me will...

You said to follow Your Torah so that I and my seed...shall...live
Following Your Torah is death to my ways
Death to my thoughts
Death to my desires...that my seed shall live
That...Your purpose in me lives...that
Your promise is fulfilled...that
Your Emet (Truth) rise up in me and that
Your Word rise up in me and that
I die to this world this
Carnivorous and
Insatiable pulling ends...dies...flesh out

Competition- cease
People pleasing- flat line
Comparison- shrink back
Negotiations with the enemy...No deal

I was not there when You called the thunder to sound and
Nor was I there when You gave the stars their names and
I was not yet found when the boarders were placed at the shores
so
I am silenced before You

I am humbled before You like
Lowly peasants before kings and
Knowing the life is in Your blood I Drink.

I now discern the Lords death...
I too must take of this cup as I break this body this Flesh.
I know now how to die...on and for purpose.
Any man that tries to save his life shall lose it Yet if he give it
up willingly Yet shall he live.

Submission Song

His sweet song swings me low...oh...
His sweet song swings me so low..yes.

His sweet song sends me to His feet, yes I will bow
down- to Him
For He is the I AM.

Ani dodi V'dodi lee
I am my beloved's and
My beloved is mine.

He sings over me and covers me under His Shadow
like none other He- is just-like
none other He- is the I Am.
He browses among the lilies like soft and sweet He is and
I am stripped of all my stubbornness and my
defiance and own way-my- own mind and I
can't help but to see His way and...

My lover is mine and I am His.
His bride made clean
His bride made clean

His bride- I am- clean.

Wisk away old troubles and double dare ya's of rebellion
just Send a wind of ready or not.
You are here just
Let me endure so I can have that white stone with my new
name and
I am victorious through blood stains and painful stripes
yes.

Tame the tongue of regret and still my heart for sin
and let it beat for repentance and change of tone
When
I die I am not alone for I am raised with You.
Yeshua the Way of Truth.

Captivate me with that song cuz
I just want to be in that number that cannot be numbered
for Eternity with Thee, Oh King of kings.

If precious is the death of all His saints then kill this flesh
Purge and dismantle flesh till there is nothing left but Your
Word.
All of You and none of me- please sing.

Sweet song of deliverance to me
Sweet songs of deliverance over my family
Sweet songs of submission till all are made clean Your
banner over me is love and Your hand is just a breath
away...

Not far away- not far away- Love is just a word away-That close.

Keep my feet on the righteous Path
Cleanse continually Your word I use as my bath Water.
If precious is the death of all Your saints then kill this flesh
And raise up my spirit as You forgive my debts.

Sing me down to Your beautiful
Sing me down to Your feet
Sing me down the isle, Lord
Make my garments white and my life complete. Sing.

Shalom,

Prophet (Nabiyah) © 2010